Level 4 Diploma in Accounting
Business Tax
Finance Act 2011

Third edition July 2011
First edition July 2010
ISBN 9781 4453 7876 3
Previous ISBN 9780 7517 8682 8

British Library Cataloguing-in-Publication Data

A catalogue record for this book is available from the British Library

Published by

BPP Learning Media Ltd, BPP House, Aldine Place, London W12 8AA

www.bpp.com/learningmedia

Printed in the United Kingdom

Your learning materials, published by BPP Learning Media Ltd,
are printed on paper sourced from sustainable, managed forests.

Welcome to BPP Learning Media's AAT **Passcards for Business Tax.**

- They **save you time**. Important topics are summarised for you.

- They incorporate **diagrams** to kick start your memory.

- They follow the overall **structure** of the BPP Learning Media Text, but BPP Learning Media's AAT **Passcards** are not just a condensed book. Each card has been separately designed for clear presentation. Topics are self contained and can be grasped visually.

- AAT **Passcards** are still **just the right size** for pockets, briefcases and bags.

- AAT **Passcards** focus on the assessment that you will be facing.

Run through the complete set of **Passcards** as often as you can in the weeks leading up to your assessment. The day before the assessment, try to go through the **Passcards** again! You will then be well on your way to assessment success.

Good luck!

Contents

The BPP Learning Media **Question Bank** contains tasks and assessments that provide invaluable practice in the skills you need to complete your assessment successfully.

1: The tax framework

Topic List

Tax law and guidance

Types of income

Total/net/taxable income

Tax computation

In Business Tax, you need an awareness of the law and guidance relevant to tax. You are expected to have a broad knowledge of how to compute an individual's income tax liability. This will allow you to give the best advice on the utilisation of business losses. However, income tax computations will not be required in Business Tax as they are assessed in Personal Tax.

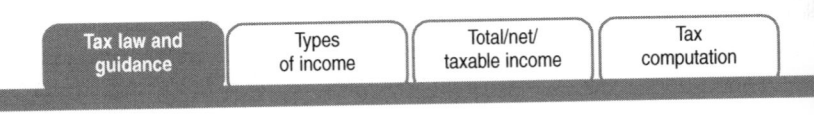

Tax law

- Statute Law: Acts of Parliament
- Case Law

■———■ Detailed regulations in Statutory Instruments (SIs)

Does not have force of law ■

HMRC Guidance

- Statements of practice
- Extra statutory concessions
- Leaflets
- Revenue and Customs Briefs
- Manuals
- Working Together

An individual may receive various types of income:

- Income from his business (trading income)
- Bank and building society interest
- Property income
- Dividends

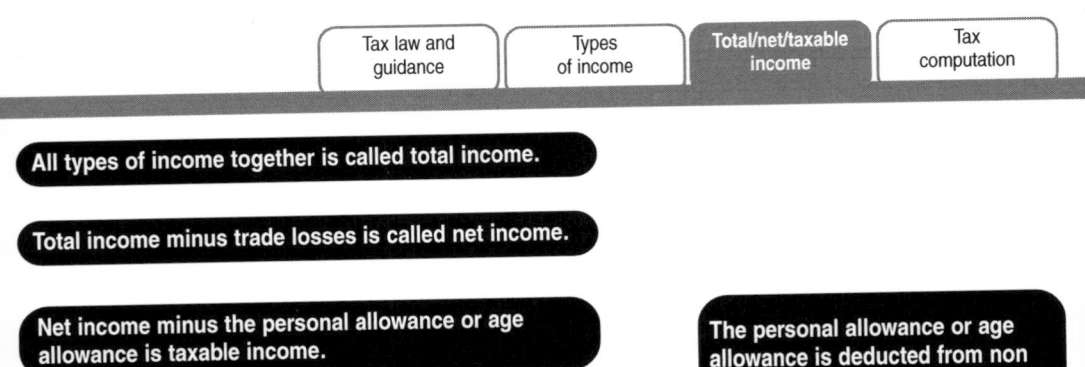

All types of income together is called total income.

Total income minus trade losses is called net income.

Net income minus the personal allowance or age allowance is taxable income.

The personal allowance or age allowance is deducted from non savings income first, then savings income and then dividend income.

Personal allowance (£7,475, 2011/12)

to age 64; taxpayers 65+ have age allowance instead of personal allowance

The personal allowance is gradually withdrawn if total income > £100,000. If total income ≥ £114,950 personal allowance = £nil.

Layout

1. Total non-savings, savings (broadly, interest) and dividend income separately.
2. Deduct the personal allowance or age allowance first from non-savings, then from savings and then from dividend income.

Savings income starting rate only applies if non-savings income is less than £2,560 (2011/12).

Taxing income

- Non-savings income is taxed first, then savings income, then dividend income is taxed last.
- Non-savings income is taxed at 20% (basic rate), then 40% (higher rate), then 50% (additional rate).
- Savings income is taxed at 10% (savings income starting rate), then 20% (basic rate), then 40% (higher rate), then 50% (additional rate).
- Dividend income within the basic rate tax band is taxed at 10% (not 20%) then at 32.5% (higher rate), then 42.5% (additional rate).

Notes

2: Capital allowances

Topic List

Capital allowances are given instead of depreciation, but they are only available for certain classes of asset. They are a trading expense deducted in arriving at Taxable Trading Profits.

Plant is apparatus that performs a function in the business.

Items that are plant

- Moveable office partitioning
- Special display lighting in retail premises
- Decorative assets used to create ambience, eg in hotel
- Cars, vans, lorries
- Furniture
- Computers

Items that are not plant

- Fixed office partitioning
- General lighting used in retail premises

Capital allowance computations

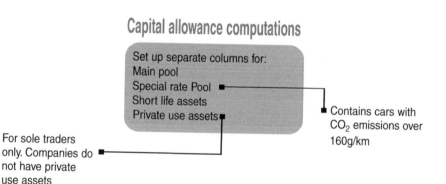

Set up separate columns for:
Main pool
Special rate Pool ■
Short life assets
Private use assets ■

■ Contains cars with CO_2 emissions over 160g/km

For sole traders only. Companies do not have private use assets

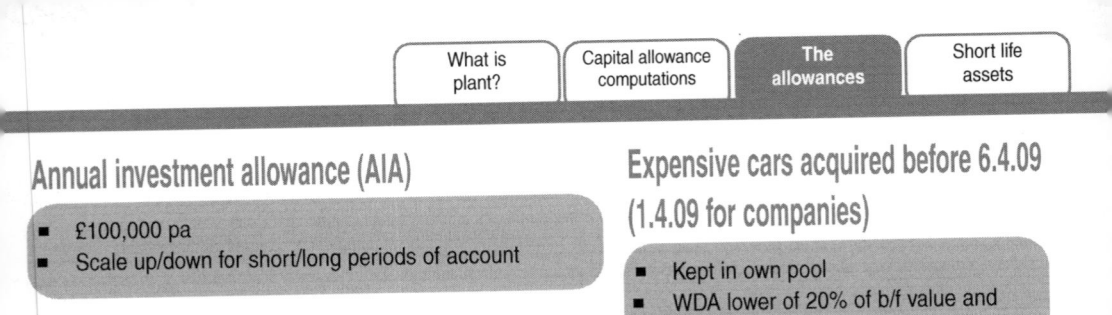

Annual investment allowance (AIA)

- £100,000 pa
- Scale up/down for short/long periods of account

Writing down allowances (WDAs)

- 20% pa in main pool on a reducing balance basis
- 10% pa in special rate pool
- 10%/20% × months/12 in short/long periods of account
- Reduced WDAs can be claimed

Expensive cars acquired before 6.4.09 (1.4.09 for companies)

- Kept in own pool
- WDA lower of 20% of b/f value and £3,000 pa

100% First year allowance (FYA)

- Available on low emission cars and energy/ water saving plant
- **Not** pro-rated in short/long periods

Cars with CO_2 emissions $\leq$ 110g/km

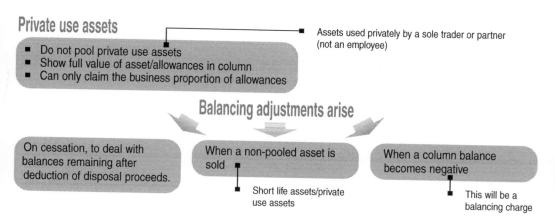

Private use assets

Assets used privately by a sole trader or partner (not an employee)

- Do not pool private use assets
- Show full value of asset/allowances in column
- Can only claim the business proportion of allowances

Balancing adjustments arise

On cessation, to deal with balances remaining after deduction of disposal proceeds.

When a non-pooled asset is sold

Short life assets/private use assets

When a column balance becomes negative

This will be a balancing charge

Short life assets (SLA)

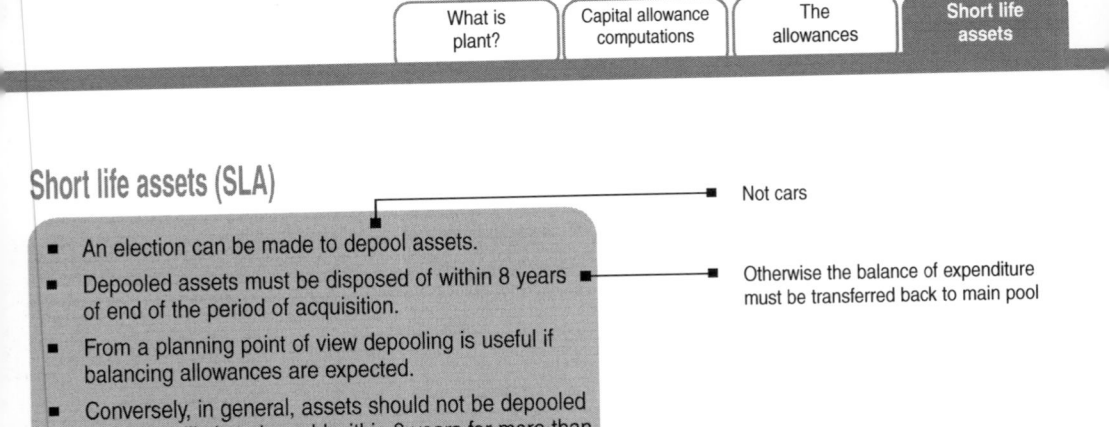

- An election can be made to depool assets.
- Depooled assets must be disposed of within 8 years of end of the period of acquisition.
- From a planning point of view depooling is useful if balancing allowances are expected.
- Conversely, in general, assets should not be depooled if they are likely to be sold within 8 years for more than their tax written down values.

■ Not cars

■ Otherwise the balance of expenditure must be transferred back to main pool

3: Computing trading income

Topic List

Badges of trade

Allowable and disallowable expenditure

In this chapter we will look at the badges of trade and at the computation of Taxable Trading Profits.

You are extremely likely to need to adjust the accounts profit for tax purposes in your assessment. The best way to become proficient at this is to practise as many adjustments as you can.

Badges of trade

- The subject matter
- The frequency of transactions
- The length of ownership
- Supplementary work and marketing
- A profit motive
- The way in which the asset sold was acquired
- The taxpayer's intentions

If, on applying the badges of trade, HMRC conclude that a trade is being carried on, the profits are taxable as Trading Profits.

To arrive at Taxable Trading Profits, the accounts profit must be adjusted. We look at this in the rest of this chapter.

Certain items of expenditure are not allowable for Taxable Trading Profit purposes, and so must be added back to the accounts profit when computing such profits. Conversely other items are allowable.

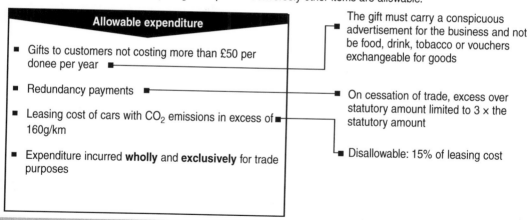

Allowable expenditure

- Gifts to customers not costing more than £50 per donee per year ▪ ─────────── The gift must carry a conspicuous advertisement for the business and not be food, drink, tobacco or vouchers exchangeable for goods

- Redundancy payments ▪ ─────────── On cessation of trade, excess over statutory amount limited to 3 × the statutory amount

- Leasing cost of cars with CO_2 emissions in excess of 160g/km ▪ ─────────── Disallowable: 15% of leasing cost

- Expenditure incurred **wholly** and **exclusively** for trade purposes

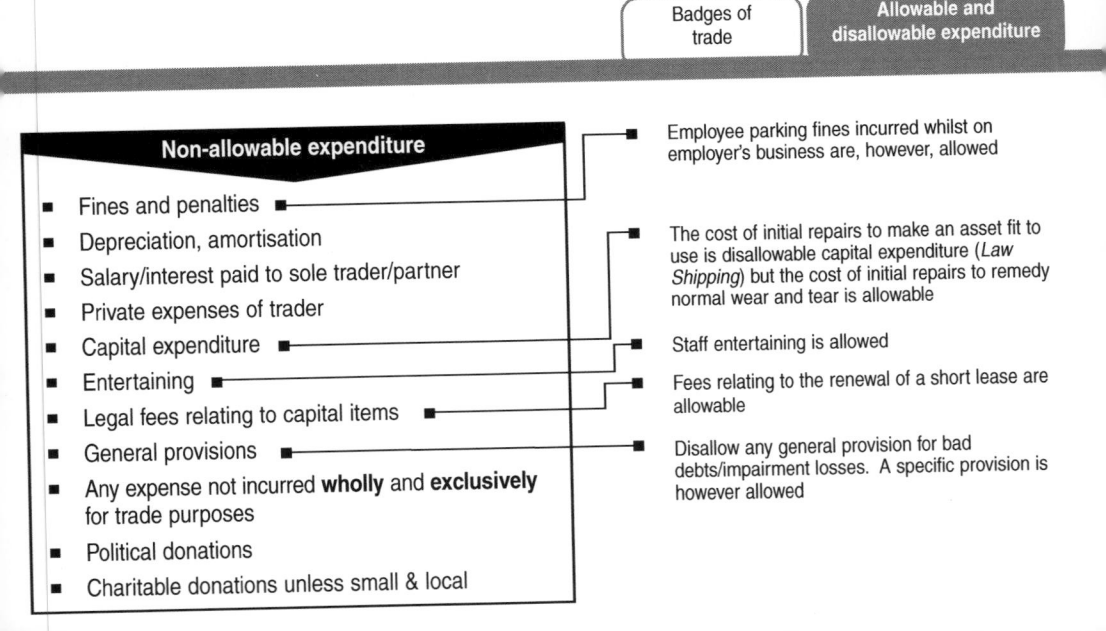

Non-allowable expenditure

- Fines and penalties ■
- Depreciation, amortisation
- Salary/interest paid to sole trader/partner
- Private expenses of trader
- Capital expenditure ■
- Entertaining ■
- Legal fees relating to capital items ■
- General provisions ■
- Any expense not incurred **wholly** and **exclusively** for trade purposes
- Political donations
- Charitable donations unless small & local

Employee parking fines incurred whilst on employer's business are, however, allowed

The cost of initial repairs to make an asset fit to use is disallowable capital expenditure (*Law Shipping*) but the cost of initial repairs to remedy normal wear and tear is allowable

Staff entertaining is allowed

Fees relating to the renewal of a short lease are allowable

Disallow any general provision for bad debts/impairment losses. A specific provision is however allowed

4: Taxing unincorporated businesses

Topic List

Continuing business

Opening years

Overlap profits

Final year

The basis period rules are the rules whereby the profits of a period of account are linked to tax years.

These rules are vitally important for the purposes of the assessment and you must make sure you know them.

The basis period for each tax year is normally the period of account ending in that tax year.

Example

A sole trader makes up accounts to 31 December each year. The basis period for 2011/12 will be the year to 31 December 2011.

There are special basis period rules in opening and closing years.

Opening years

Year	1	2 more than	3
Basis period	Date of commencement – 5 April following.	If the accounting date in year 2 is 12 months long, the 12 months to that date. If the accounting date in year 2 is less than 12 months long, the first 12 months of trading. If there is no accounting date in year 2, the year itself (6/4 – 5/4).	12 months to accounting date in year 3.

Any profits taxed twice in the opening years are called overlap profits.

➡️

Overlap profits may be relieved on cessation.

Assessment focus

You can easily check any computation that stretches over the whole life of a business. The total taxable profits (less losses) should equal the total actual profits (less actual losses).

Final year

Overlap profits are deducted from the final year's profits.

profits as adjusted for tax

Final year

The basis period for the final year starts at the end of the basis period for the previous year, and ends at cessation.

Example

Nitin, who has been trading for many years, prepares accounts to 30 June each year. Overlap profits of £9,000 arose when Nitin started trading. Results for recent years have been:

| y/e 30.6.10 | £50,000 |
| y/e 30.6.11 | £70,000 |

On 30.9.11 Nitin ceased trading. Profits for the three months to 30.9.11 were £15,000. What is Nitin's final Trading Profit assessment?

The trade ends in 2011/12 so 2011/12 is the final year ■

The basis period for 2010/11 would have been the y/e 30.6.10. The basis period for 2011/12 therefore runs from 1.7.10 ■

Overlap profits are deducted from the final year's assessment ■

Solution

2011/12 is the final year of trade.

The basis period is the period 1.7.10 - 30.9.11.

The assessment for 2011/12 is:

	£
y/e 30.6.11	70,000
3 m/e 30.9.11	15,000
Less: overlap profits	(9,000)
	76,000

Notes

Topic List

Sharing profits between partners

A partnership's results are computed in the same way as the results of a sole trader. Once the results are found, they can then be allocated to individual partners.

1	Compute Taxable Trading Profits for a partnership as a whole in the same way as you would compute the profits for a sole trader, then	This means starting with the accounts profit and adding back disallowables/deducting amounts specifically deductible under the tax rules.
2	Divide results for each period of account between partners	When a partner joins, the first period of account for his own business runs from the date of joining to the firm's next accounting date. The normal basis period rules for opening years apply to him.
3	Tax each partner as if he were running his own business, and making profits and losses equal to his share of the firm's results for each period of account	When a partner leaves, the last period of account for his own business runs from the firm's most recent accounting date to the day he leaves. The normal cessation rules apply to him.

Dividing results of each period of account between partners:

1 First, allocate salaries and interest on capital. ■————————■ Remember to pro-rate the annual salary/interest if the period concerned is not 12 months long.

2 Second, share the balance of the firm's results among the partners according to the profit-sharing arrangement for the period of account.

Example

Tim and Patrick are in partnership. They take annual salaries of £10,000 each, and thereafter share profits 60% to Tim and 40% to Patrick. Profits of £100,000 were made in the six months to 30 September 2011. Show what amount is allocated to each partner.

	Tim £	Patrick £	Total £
Salary (6/12)	5,000	5,000	10,000
Balance	54,000	36,000	90,000
	59,000	41,000	100,000

6: Losses

There is no general rule that sole traders can get relief for their losses. The conditions of a specific relief must be complied with. We look at these reliefs in this chapter.

A Trading Loss in a basis period is calculated in exactly the same way as a Taxable Trading Profit would be. The loss must then be allocated to the correct tax year. Eg. A loss for y/end 31.12.11 would be allocated to 2011/12.

Carry forward

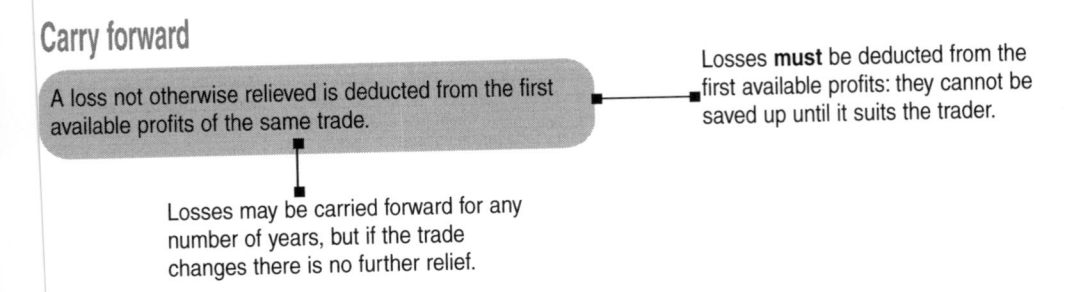

A loss not otherwise relieved is deducted from the first available profits of the same trade.

Losses **must** be deducted from the first available profits: they cannot be saved up until it suits the trader.

Losses may be carried forward for any number of years, but if the trade changes there is no further relief.

Relief

Loss is deducted from total income of the tax year of the loss and/or the preceding tax year.

Partial claims are not allowed; the whole loss must be deducted, so far as there is income available to absorb it in the chosen tax year of relief.

Example

Sue makes up accounts to 30 September. Recent results are:

y/e 30.9.11	£(50,000)
y/e 30.9.12	£25,000

Results for the tax years are:

2011/12	£(50,000):	Loss
2012/13	£25,000:	Profit

Assessment focus

Before recommending this relief, consider whether it would lead to the waste of the personal allowance. This is often a significant tax planning point.

7: National Insurance

NICs for the self-employed

In this chapter we look at NICs paid by the self-employed.

These are the only NICs that are assessable.

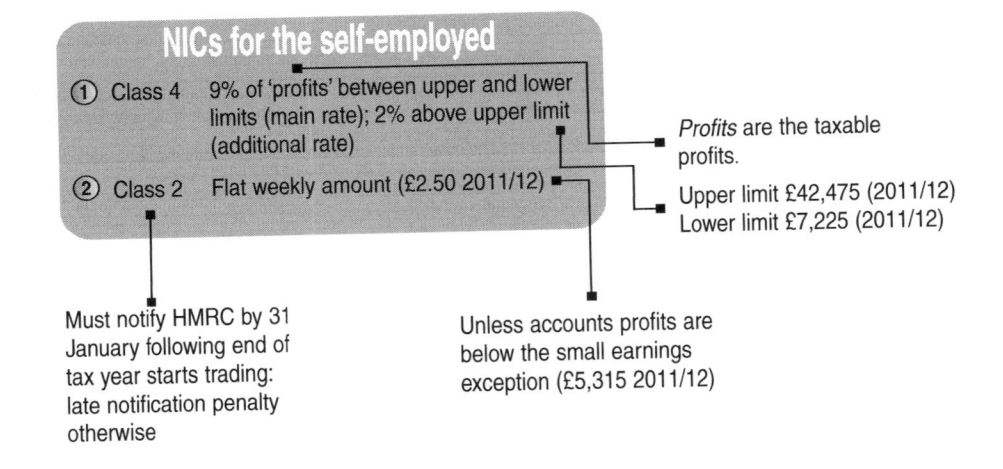

NICs for the self-employed

① Class 4 — 9% of 'profits' between upper and lower limits (main rate); 2% above upper limit (additional rate)

② Class 2 — Flat weekly amount (£2.50 2011/12)

Profits are the taxable profits.

Upper limit £42,475 (2011/12)
Lower limit £7,225 (2011/12)

Must notify HMRC by 31 January following end of tax year starts trading: late notification penalty otherwise

Unless accounts profits are below the small earnings exception (£5,315 2011/12)

8: Self assessment for individuals

Topic List

Returns

Records

Payment of tax

Interest and late payment of tax

Enquiries

This chapter looks at when returns must be filed and at due dates for the payment of tax.

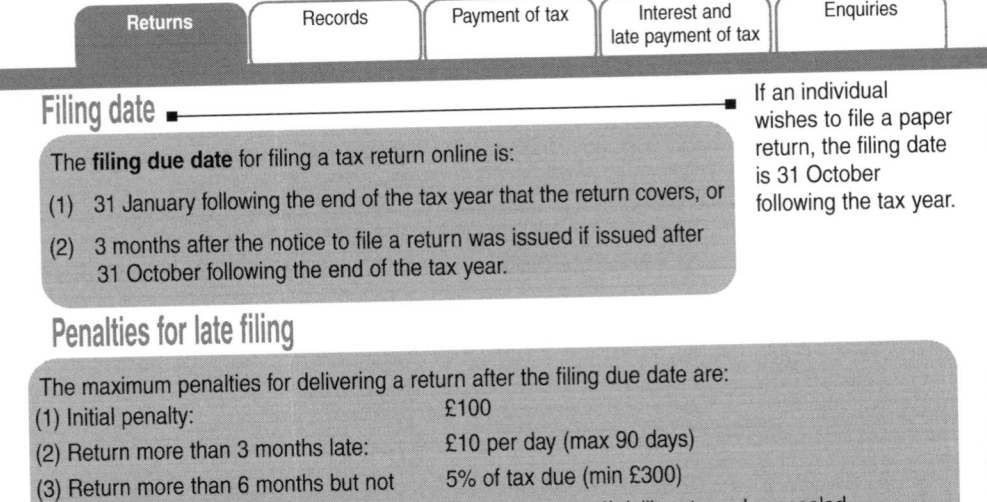

Filing date

The **filing due date** for filing a tax return online is:

(1) 31 January following the end of the tax year that the return covers, or

(2) 3 months after the notice to file a return was issued if issued after 31 October following the end of the tax year.

If an individual wishes to file a paper return, the filing date is 31 October following the tax year.

Penalties for late filing

The maximum penalties for delivering a return after the filing due date are:

(1) Initial penalty:	£100
(2) Return more than 3 months late:	£10 per day (max 90 days)
(3) Return more than 6 months but not more than 12 months late:	5% of tax due (min £300)
(4) Return more than 12 months late:	100% of tax due if deliberate and concealed
	70% of tax due if deliberate but not concealed
	5% of tax due, otherwise (min £300 each case) (eg careless)

Penalties for error

Imposed if inaccurate return for:

- Carelessness
- Deliberate error but no arrangements to conceal
- Deliberate error and arrangements to conceal

Amount of penalty

PLR is Potential Lost Revenue eg tax unpaid

Reduced if error disclosed to HMRC

	Maximum of PLR	Minimum of PLR	
		Unprompted	Prompted
Careless	30%	0%	15%
Deliberate, not concealed	70%	20%	35%
Deliberate, concealed	100%	30%	50%

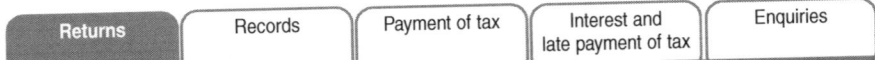
Penalties for late notification

Imposed if does not notify chargeability by 5 October following end of tax year

Amount of penalty

| | Maximum of PLR | Minimum of PLR | |
		Unprompted	Prompted
Careless	30%	>12m <12m 10% 0%	>12m <12m 20% 10%
Deliberate but not concealed	70%	20%	35%
Deliberate and concealed	100%	30%	50%

Records

Records must, in general, be kept until the later of:

(1) 5 years after the 31 January following the tax year concerned (where the taxpayer is in business or has rental income); or

(2) 1 year after the 31 January following the tax year, otherwise.

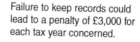

Failure to keep records could lead to a penalty of £3,000 for each tax year concerned.

Payment of tax

Payments on account (POA) of income tax and Class 4 NICs must be made on 31 January in tax year and on the following 31 July.

The final payment of income tax must be paid on 31 January following the tax year.

Class 2 NIC is paid in two instalments on 31 January and 31 July

Payments on account

1. Each POA is 50% of the prior tax year's liability less tax suffered at source

2. POAs are not required if the relevant amount falls below £1,000 or more than 80% of prior year liability met at source

3. A claim may be made to reduce POAs to a stated amount, or nil

Late payment of tax

Penalties are levied on late payment of a final payment of income tax, Class 4 NICs or CGT as follows:

Paid	Penalty
(1) Within 30 days of due date	none
(2) Not more than six months after due date	5% of tax due
(3) More than six months but not more than twelve months after due date	further 5% of tax due
(4) More than twelve months after due date	further 5% of tax due

Interest

Interest runs on:

(1) POAs from the normal due dates (31 Jan and 31 July).

(2) Any final payment, and CGT, from the later of:

31 January following tax year

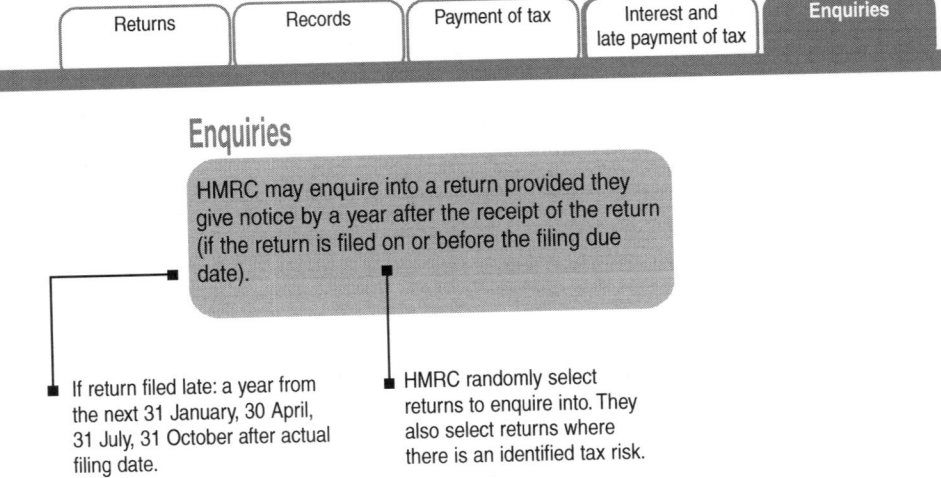

Enquiries

HMRC may enquire into a return provided they give notice by a year after the receipt of the return (if the return is filed on or before the filing due date).

If return filed late: a year from the next 31 January, 30 April, 31 July, 31 October after actual filing date.

HMRC randomly select returns to enquire into. They also select returns where there is an identified tax risk.

9: Computing taxable total profits

Companies pay corporation tax rather than income tax or CGT.

In this chapter we will cover how taxable total profits are computed. This is likely to be an essential part of your assessment.

A company's taxable total profits are arrived at by aggregating its various sources of income and chargeable gains and then deducting Gift Aid donations.

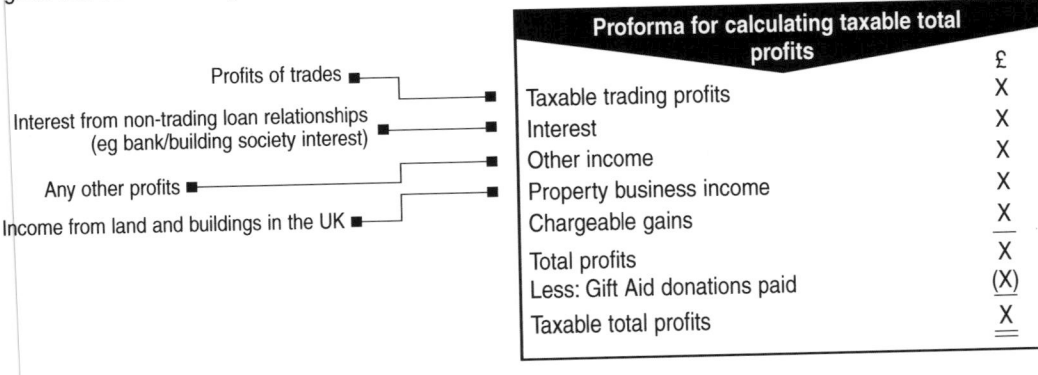

	£
Proforma for calculating taxable total profits	
Taxable trading profits	X
Interest	X
Other income	X
Property business income	X
Chargeable gains	X
Total profits	X
Less: Gift Aid donations paid	(X)
Taxable total profits	X

Profits of trades ■

Interest from non-trading loan relationships ■
(eg bank/building society interest)

Any other profits ■

Income from land and buildings in the UK ■

Dividends from other companies are not included in taxable total profits.

Property business income

All property business income is treated as a single source of income, calculated in the same way as trading profits.

You will not be expected to compute property business income in Business Tax, but you may be expected to include the income in arriving at taxable total profits.

Companies must pay corporation tax on their **taxable total profits** in each **accounting period**.

An accounting period can never exceed 12 months. If a company prepares accounts for a period exceeding twelve months, this period of account must be split into two accounting periods.

| The first 12 months form the first accounting period | The remaining months form the second accounting period |

Example

If A Ltd prepares accounts for the fifteen months to 31.12.11, there will be one 12 month accounting period to 30.9.11 and a second 3 month accounting period to 31.12.11.

Long period of account

If a period of account exceeds 12 months, divide profits between the accounting periods as follows:

- Trading income: time apportion the amount before capital allowances
- Compute capital allowances separately for each period
- Interest income: allocate to the period in which it accrues
- Property business income and other income: time apportion
- Gains: allocate to the period in which they are realised
- Gift Aid donations: allocate to the period in which paid

10: Computing corporation tax payable

Topic List

Rates of corporation tax

Upper and lower limits

The rate of corporation tax is set for financial years.
There are special rates for smaller companies.

Rates

Rates of corporation tax (CT) are:

- Set for financial years
- Dependent on the level of augmented profits

A financial year runs from 1 April in one year to 31 March in the next. **Financial year 2011 (FY 2011) runs from 1 April 2011 to 31 March 2012.**

If there is a change in the rate of CT, and a company's accounting period does not fall entirely into one financial year, the taxable total profits of the period is time apportioned to the two financial years, when calculating the tax.

Augmented profits are taxable total profits plus the grossed up amount of dividends received from UK companies.

ignore dividends from associated companies.

The **main rate** (FY 2011: 26%) of CT applies if augmented profits exceed the upper limit.

The **small profits rate** (SPR) (FY 2011: 20%) applies if augmented profits are below the lower limit.

Marginal relief is given if augmented profits fall between the upper and lower limits

Assessment focus

The marginal relief formula will be given to you in your assessment.

It is (marginal relief standard fraction) × (upper limit – augmented profits) × $\dfrac{\text{Taxable total profits}}{\text{Augmented profits}}$

Profits between upper & lower limits **effectively** taxed at 27.5%. Not an actual tax rate.

Upper and lower limits

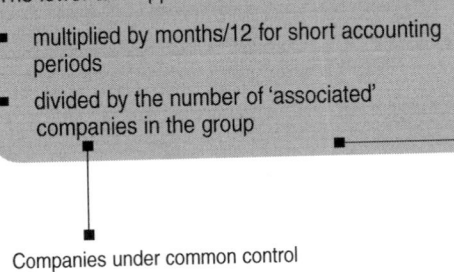

The lower and upper limits are:

- multiplied by months/12 for short accounting periods
- divided by the number of 'associated' companies in the group

Companies under common control

Exclude dormant companies but include trading non-resident companies

Example

A Ltd, which has one associated company, prepares accounts for the nine months to 31.3.11. The upper limit for this period is
$$9/12 \times \frac{£1,500,000}{2} = £562,500$$

11: Chargeable gains for companies

Topic List

Chargeable persons, disposals and assets

Computing gains and losses

Part disposals

Chattels

Companies pay corporation tax on their chargeable gains.

We look at the basic rules applicable to chargeable gains and then some specific rules applying to part disposals and chattels.

Chargeable persons, disposals and assets

Three elements are needed for a chargeable gain to arise:

 A **chargeable disposal**: this includes sales, gifts and the destruction of assets.

A **chargeable person**: companies and individuals.

 A **chargeable asset**: most assets are chargeable; exempt assets include cars and some chattels (eg racehorses).

Computation

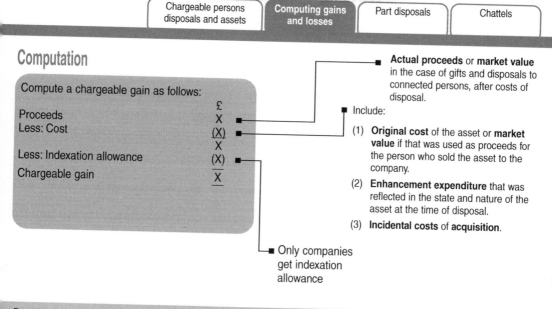

Compute a chargeable gain as follows:

	£
Proceeds	X
Less: Cost	(X)
	X
Less: Indexation allowance	(X)
Chargeable gain	X

- **Actual proceeds** or **market value** in the case of gifts and disposals to connected persons, after costs of disposal.

- Include:

  (1) **Original cost** of the asset or **market value** if that was used as proceeds for the person who sold the asset to the company.

  (2) **Enhancement expenditure** that was reflected in the state and nature of the asset at the time of disposal.

  (3) **Incidental costs** of **acquisition**.

- Only companies get indexation allowance

Indexation allowance

- Expenditure times indexation factor
- Runs from date of acquisition to date of disposal on acquisition cost (and costs of acquisition)
- Runs from date incurred to date of disposal on enhancement expenditure
- Does not apply to disposal costs

Indexation factor

Will be given to you in assessment

Losses

Indexation allowance cannot create or increase an allowable loss

Part disposals

On a part disposal, you are only allowed to take part of the cost of the asset into account.

- Costs attributable solely to the part disposed of are taken into account in full
- For other costs, take into account A/(A+B) of the cost
  - A is the proceeds of the part sold
  - B is the market value of the part retained

Example

X Ltd owns land that originally cost £30,000. It sold a quarter interest in the land for £18,000. The incidental costs of disposal were £1,000. The market value of the three-quarter share remaining is estimated to be £36,000. What is the chargeable gain? Ignore indexation allowance.

	£
Proceeds	18,000
Less: Incidental costs of disposal	(1,000)
Less: $\dfrac{18,000}{18,000 + 36,000} \times 30,000$	(10,000)
Chargeable gain	7,000

Chattels

A chattel is an item of **tangible moveable property** (eg a painting).

Gains on chattels sold for gross proceeds of £6,000 or less and on wasting chattels are **exempt**.

Remaining useful life of 50 years or less (eg racehorse)

The maximum gain on chattels sold for more than £6,000 is **5/3 (gross proceeds − £6,000)**.

Losses on chattels sold for under £6,000 are restricted by **assuming the gross proceeds to be £6,000**.

12: Share disposals by companies

The computation of gains or losses on the disposal of shares by a company is a key topic for your assessment.

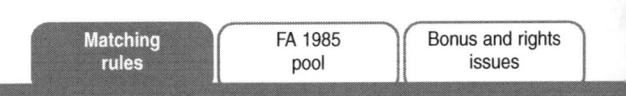

Shares of one class in one company are identical, but they may have been bought at different times, for different prices. We therefore need matching rules to work out the cost of shares sold.

Matching
Disposals by company shareholders are matched with acquisitions in the following order:
▪ Shares acquired on the same day
▪ Shares acquired in the previous nine days, taking earlier acquisitions first
▪ Shares from the FA 1985 pool ▪

- ▪ Shares acquired after 31 March 1982

- ▪ Pool starts on 1 April 1985 with costs plus indexation to then

- ▪ Indexation runs to date of disposal of shares

Where shares are disposed of within nine days of acquisition, no indexation allowance is available even if the acquisition and the disposal fall in different months. Acquisitions matched with disposals under the nine day rule never enter the FA 1985 pool.

The FA 1985 pool is kept in 3 columns:

1 The **number** of shares

2 The **cost**

3 The **indexed cost** ■

This starts at 1 April 1985 with the cost of acquisitions plus indexation to that date

Operative events are acquisitions and disposals (apart from bonus issues).

At each operative event:

(1) Increase the indexed cost column by the indexed rise since the date of the last operative event, then

(2) Add the cost of any shares acquired to both the cost/indexed cost columns, or

The indexation allowance is the indexed cost taken from the indexed cost column minus the cost taken from the cost column

■ (3) Deduct a pro-rata slice from the cost/indexed cost columns in respect of any shares disposed of.

Bonus issues

- Bonus issues relating to the FA 1985 pool go into that pool.
- Simply add the number of shares to FA 1985 pool; there is no cost.

Rights issues

Rights issues relating to FA 1985 pool shares are treated as an operative event. Index the pool to the date of the rights issue and then add in the cost and number of rights issue shares.

13: Corporation tax losses

Topic List

Trading losses

Other losses

In this chapter we will see how a company may obtain tax relief for its trading losses.

For the assessment, the best way of learning how to deal with losses is to practise as many tasks involving losses as you can.

The methods of relieving losses for a company are different from the methods of relief for an individual. Do not confuse the two.

Trading losses are the losses made by a company in its trade.

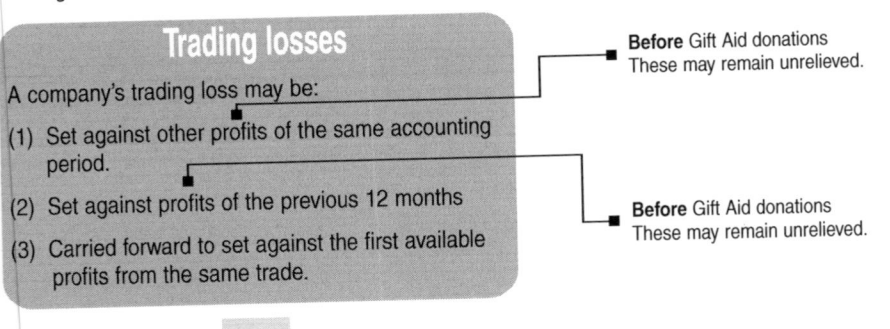

Trading losses

A company's trading loss may be:

(1) Set against other profits of the same accounting period.

(2) Set against profits of the previous 12 months

(3) Carried forward to set against the first available profits from the same trade.

Before Gift Aid donations
These may remain unrelieved.

Before Gift Aid donations
These may remain unrelieved.

- Reliefs (1) and (2) must be claimed
- A company can choose to claim relief (1) only
- If relief (2) is to be claimed, relief (1) must be claimed first
- Relief (3) is given automatically to any loss not relieved under (1) or (2)

Tax planning

- Aim to relieve losses against profits suffering the highest marginal tax rate
- Also consider the timing of relief and the extent to which any Gift Aid donations become unrelieved

13: Corporation tax losses

Capital losses

- Only set against current or future gains, never income
- Cannot be carried back

Property business losses

- Set off against other income/gains for current period
- Excess carried forward as property business loss of future accounting period

14: Self assessment for companies

Topic List

Returns

Payment of tax

In this chapter we look at both the administration of corporation tax (CT) and at when that tax must be paid. As the due dates for payment of CT impact on a company's cash flow position, it is vitally important to be aware of these dates.

Returns

A company must normally file its CT return by the filing due date which is the later of:

- 12 months after the end of the period to which the return relates
- 3 months after a notice requiring the return was issued

Enquiries

Notice to enquire into a return must be given by 12 months after the later of:

- the actual filing date (if filed on or before filing due date); or
- the 31 January, 30 April, 31 July or 31 October next following the actual filing date (if filed after filing due date)

Companies must file **online**

Late filing of return – as for individuals.

Penalties for error – as for individuals.

Records must generally be kept for six years from the end of the accounting period concerned.

Due dates

- 'Large' companies must pay their CT in instalments
- Other companies must pay their CT nine months and one day after the end of the accounting period (AP)

- Any company that pays CT at the main rate

Interest runs from the due date. Interest paid is a tax deductible expense for companies.

Quarterly instalments

- For a 12 month AP instalments are due in:
  - months 7 and 10 of the period
  - months 1 and 4 of the following period

- instalments due on 14th day of month concerned

Notes

15: Chargeable gains for individuals

Topic List

Basic computation

The charge to CGT

Losses

Connected persons

Spouses and civil partners

It is important that you can calculate chargeable gains realised by both sole traders and companies. The computations are similar but not identical.

This chapter is concerned with the computation of chargeable gains for individuals.

Computation

Compute a gain as follows:

	£
Proceeds	X
Less: Cost	(X)
Chargeable gain	X

Actual proceeds or **market value** in the case of gifts and disposals that are not bargains at arm's length, after costs of disposal.

Include:

(1) **Original cost** of the asset or **market value** if that was used as proceeds for the person who sold the asset to the individual.

(2) **Enhancement expenditure** reflected in the state and nature of the asset at the time of disposal.

(3) **Incidental costs** of **acquisition**.

Part disposals and chattels

Rules apply as for companies

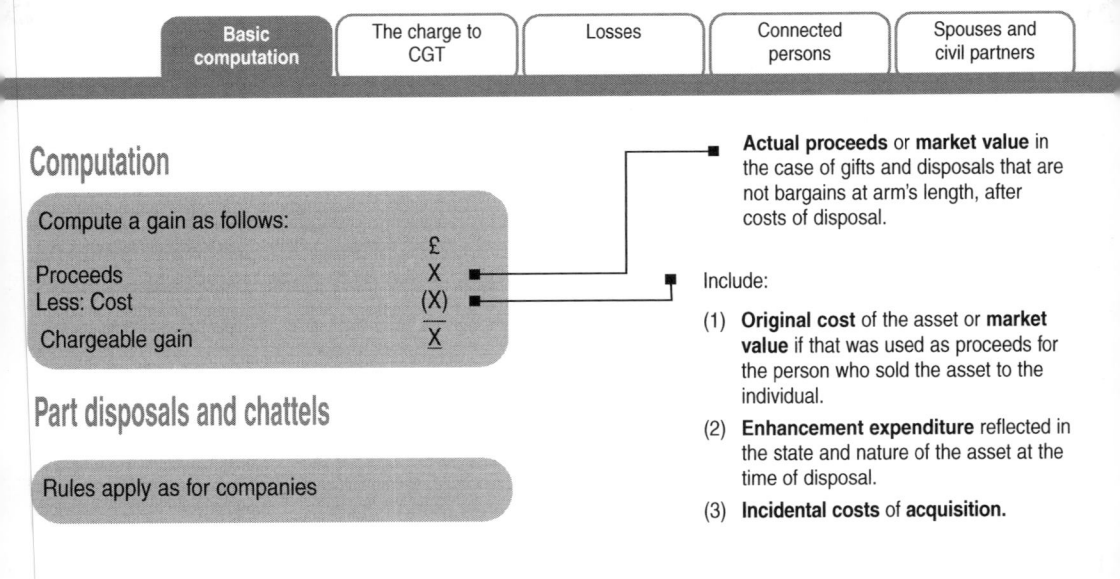

Deduct the CGT annual exempt amount of £10,600 (2011/12) when computing an individual's total taxable gains.

Rate

– 28% if higher or additional rate taxpayer

– 18% on taxable gains up to the amount of the unused basic rate band and 28% on the excess

Due date

CGT for 2011/12 is due on 31 January 2013

Example

Sue made taxable gains (after the annual exempt amount) in July 2011 of £10,000.

She has £6,000 of unused basic rate band.

What CGT must Sue pay?

She must pay CGT of £6,000 × 18% + £4,000 × 28% = £2,200

Deduct allowable capital losses from chargeable gains in the tax year in which they arise.

Any loss that cannot be set off is carried forward to set against future chargeable gains.

Allowable losses brought forward are only set off to reduce current year chargeable gains less current year allowable losses to the annual exempt amount.

Example

Zoë made gains of £12,600 in 2011/11. She had brought forward capital losses of £8,000.

Brought forward capital losses of £2,000 will be set off in 2011/12. The remaining losses will be carried forward to 2012/13.

Disposals between connected persons are deemed to be for the **market values** of the assets. If a loss arises on a disposal to a connected person it can only be set against chargeable gains on disposals to the **same** connected person.

An individual is connected with his spouse/civil partner's relatives (brothers, sisters, ancestors and lineal descendants) and their spouses/civil partners.

Exception: Does not apply to no gain/no loss disposals (see spouses and civil partners).

Spouses and civil partners

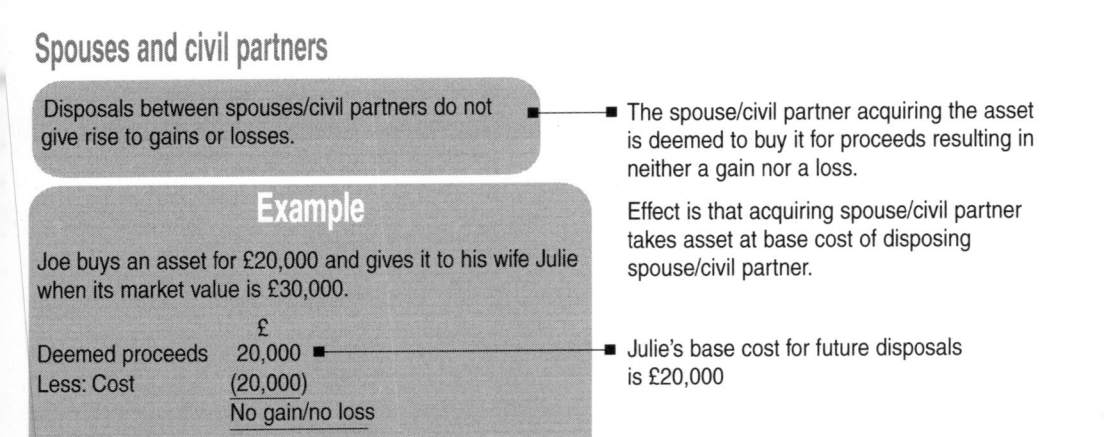

Disposals between spouses/civil partners do not give rise to gains or losses.

- The spouse/civil partner acquiring the asset is deemed to buy it for proceeds resulting in neither a gain nor a loss.

  Effect is that acquiring spouse/civil partner takes asset at base cost of disposing spouse/civil partner.

Example

Joe buys an asset for £20,000 and gives it to his wife Julie when its market value is £30,000.

	£
Deemed proceeds	20,000
Less: Cost	(20,000)
	No gain/no loss

- Julie's base cost for future disposals is £20,000

16: Share disposals by individuals

Topic List

Matching rules

Bonus and rights issues

The special rules for shares disposed of by individuals are covered in this chapter.

The matching rules for shares held by an individual are different from the matching rules for shares held by a company. Take care not to confuse the two.

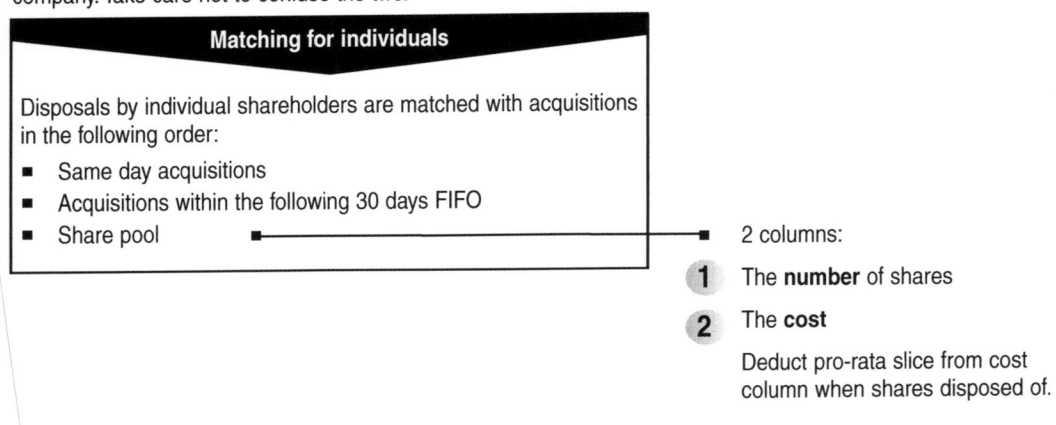

Matching for individuals

Disposals by individual shareholders are matched with acquisitions in the following order:

- Same day acquisitions
- Acquisitions within the following 30 days FIFO
- Share pool

2 columns:

1 The **number** of shares

2 The **cost**

Deduct pro-rata slice from cost column when shares disposed of.

Bonus issues

Simply add the number of shares to share pool; there is no cost

Rights issues

Add number of shares and cost to share pool

Notes

17: Reliefs for chargeable gains

Topic List

Entrepreneurs' relief

Rollover relief

Gift relief

In the assessment you should look out for the availability of various reliefs. However, do take care to ensure that you do not claim relief when you are not allowed to.

Entrepreneurs' relief reduces the rate of CGT payable on certain business assets to 10%.

Rollover relief applies for individuals and companies when certain assets used in a business are sold and other business assets purchased.

Gift relief is available on certain types of assets. You must be able to identify the assets that qualify for gift relief and discuss how the relief operates.

Conditions

Material disposal of business assets:

- Disposal of whole or part of business owned for at least one year

- Disposal of assets used for business on cessation if business owned for at least one year and disposal within three years of cessation

- Disposal of trading company shares where company is personal company and individual is officer or employee, all for at least one year

Claims

By first anniversary of 31 January following end of tax year of disposal

- Personal company: individual holds at least 5% of ordinary shares and voting rights.

How it works

- Qualifying gains taxed at 10%
- Lifetime limit of £10 million eligible gains
- Gains eligible for entrepreneurs' relief are treated as the lowest slice of gains.

Example

Chris sells his business in November 2011. The gains are £150,000. He also has another non business gain of £17,000 for 2011/12. Chris has taxable income of £30,000 for 2011/12. What is his CGT payable?

	£
Gains qualifying for entrepreneurs' relief	
£150,000 × 10%	15,000
Other gains	
(£17,000 − £10,600) × 28%	1,792
	16,792

Uses up remaining basic rate band despite being taxed at 10%

Eligible assets

Taxpayers can claim to defer gains arising on the disposal of business assets that are being replaced if both the old and the new assets are on the list of eligible assets and are used in the trade.

- Land & buildings used for the purposes of the trade
- Fixed (that is, immoveable) plant and machinery.
- Goodwill (for individuals only)

The new asset must be bought in the period starting 12 months before and ending 36 months after the disposal.

If rollover relief is claimed the deferred gain is deducted from the base cost of the new asset.

If disposal proceeds are only partially reinvested in the new asset, an amount of the gain equal to the proceeds not reinvested is immediately chargeable. The remainder of the gain can be deferred.

Example

Prianka sold land used in her business for £500,000 realising a gain of £150,000. Two months later she bought an office building for £480,000.

An amount of the gain equal to the proceeds not reinvested in the office, £20,000, is immediately chargeable. The remaining gain, £130,000 may be rolled over. The rolled over gain is deducted from the base cost of the building, which will then become £350,000 (£480,000 – £130,000).

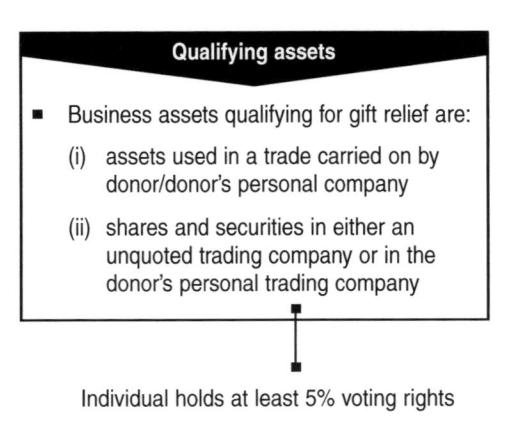

When gift relief is **claimed**, the gain on the gift is deducted from the recipient's base cost.

Qualifying assets

- Business assets qualifying for gift relief are:

  (i) assets used in a trade carried on by donor/donor's personal company

  (ii) shares and securities in either an unquoted trading company or in the donor's personal trading company

Individual holds at least 5% voting rights

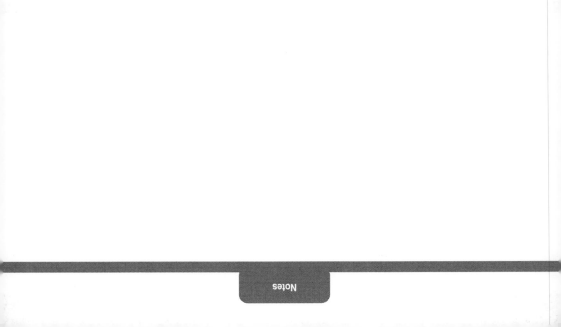

Notes

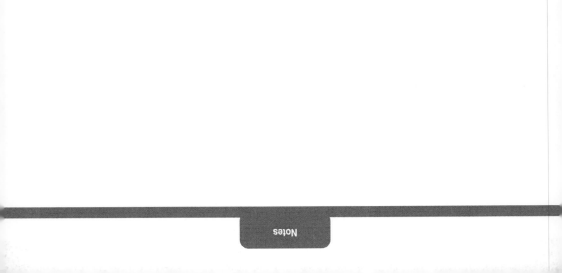
Notes

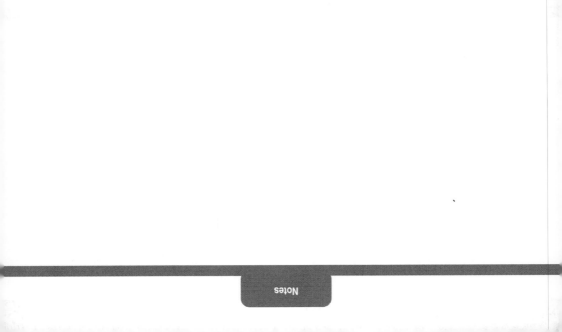

Notes

Notes

Notes

Notes